Ways into Science

Electricity

Buzz!

Written by Peter Riley

W
FRANKLIN WATTS
LONDON·SYDNEY

First published in 2001 by Franklin Watts
96 Leonard Street, London EC2A 4XD

Franklin Watts Australia
56 O'Riordan Street
Alexandria, NSW 2015

Series editor: Rachel Cooke
Assistant editor: Adrian Cole
Series design: Jason Anscomb
Design: Michael Leaman Design Partnership
Photography: Ray Moller (unless
otherwise credited)

A CIP catalogue record for this book
is available from the British Library

ISBN 0 7496 3954 7

Dewey Classification 537

Printed in Malaysia

Picture credits:
iMac courtesy of Apple Computers UK p. 6; Pictor
International p. 22tl and br
Thanks to our models:
Olivia Al-Adwani, Ammar Duffus, Russell Langer,
Gabrielle Locke, Rukaiyah Qazi, Giselle Quarrington,
Perry Robinson and Matthew Sharp

Contents

Electricity

Electricity makes
things work.

Electricity works
a Walkman.

Electricity works
a computer.

We use electricity made by batteries.

We use electricity from the mains.

Mains electricity can harm you. Take great care with it.

Batteries

Take a close look
at a battery.

It has a plus sign
on one end.
It has a minus
sign on the
other end.

A battery holder has plus and
minus signs, too.
You match plus and minus signs
when you put a battery in its place.

This torch has two batteries. They are laid end to end.

You put the plus sign of one battery next to the minus sign of the other to make the torch work.

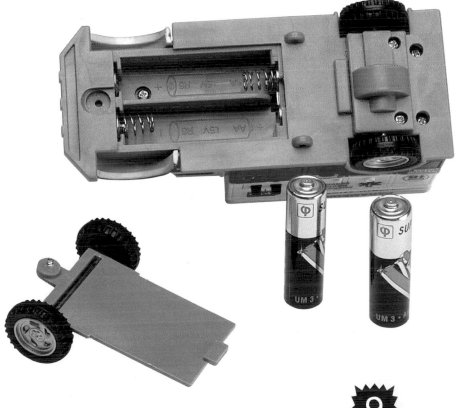

Take the batteries out of a toy that uses them. Can you put them back in again? What helps you do this?

Switches

This torch has batteries in it but it is not lit up.

You use a switch to turn electricity on and off.

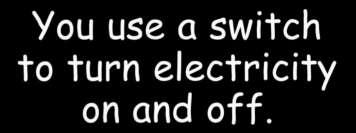

switch

You have to press the switch to make the torch work.

Toys have switches too.

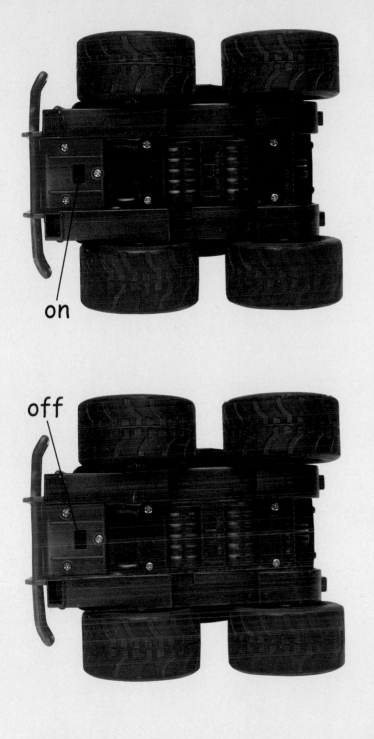

on

off

On this toy, you slide the switch one way to make it work and the other way to make it stop.

What other kind of switches do you use?

Make a circuit

Electricity works in a circle called a circuit.

Ben has got a battery in a holder, a bulb, three wires and a switch. He makes them into a circuit.

He attaches a wire to the battery.

He attaches the bulb to this wire.

He attaches the next
wire to the bulb and then
to the switch.

Finally, he uses the third
wire to attach the switch
to the battery.

What will happen when
he switches on?
Turn the page to find out.

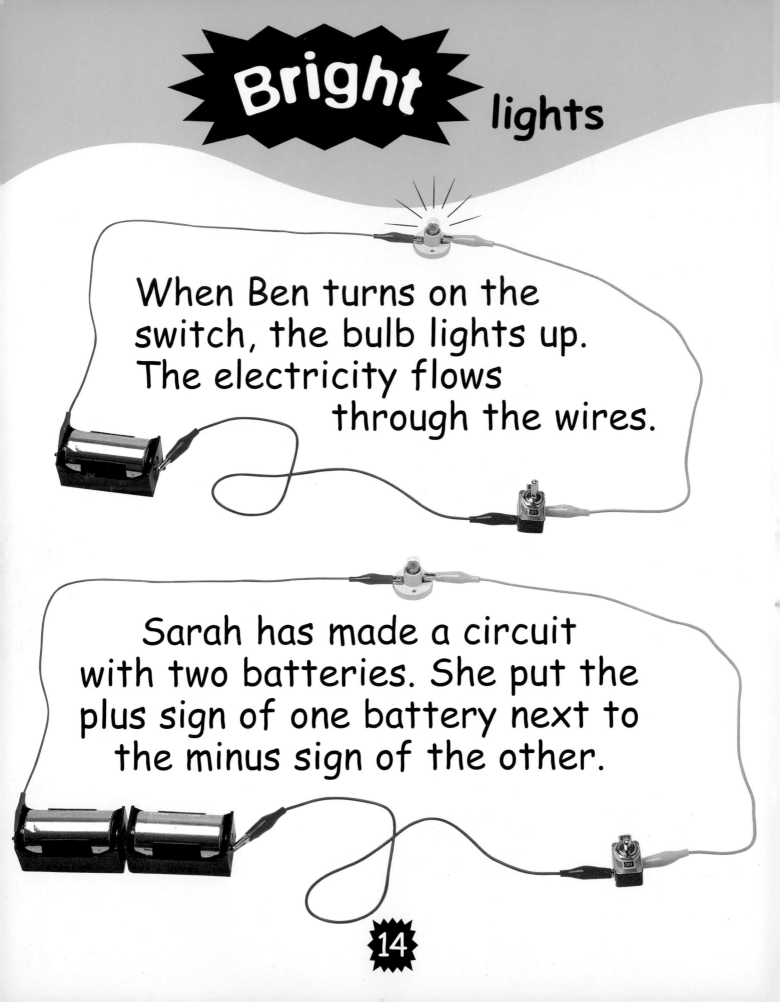

Bright lights

When Ben turns on the switch, the bulb lights up. The electricity flows through the wires.

Sarah has made a circuit with two batteries. She put the plus sign of one battery next to the minus sign of the other.

Sarah switches
her circuit on and
the bulb lights up.

Because Sarah used two
batteries, the bulb shines
brighter than Ben's bulb.

There is more electricity
flowing through the wires.

Make circuits like Ben's and Sarah's.
How could you record what you have done?

When electricity flows through an electric motor the shaft moves round.

motor

shaft

An electric motor makes this toy boat's propeller spin.

Buzzers

A buzzer makes a sound when electricity flows through it.

Some toys have buzzers in them. This ambulance has a loud buzzer.

Buzz!

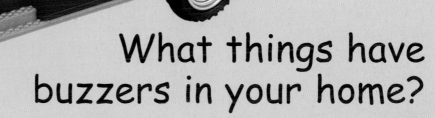

Buzz!

What things have buzzers in your home?

Kate has made
a circuit with
a motor.

She has put
a round-about on
the motor's shaft.

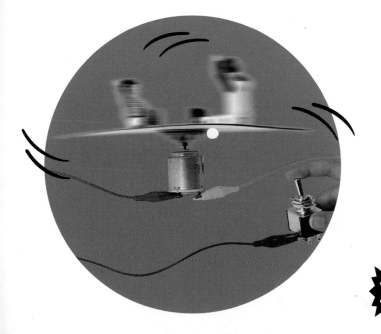

She turns on
the switch.
The round-about
spins round.

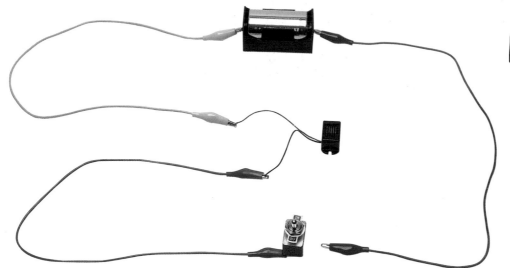

Paul has made a circuit with a buzzer in it.

He hopes to make Kate jump when he switches it on.

What do you think will happen?
Turn the page to find out.

Make it work

The buzzer does not work.

There is a gap in the circuit.

The gap stops the electricity from flowing around the circuit.

Now Paul attaches the wire to the switch. He turns on the switch.

This time Kate gets a fright!

Buzz!

Make circuits with batteries and buzzers. Why should you check them for gaps?

Mains electricity

Mains electricity is made in power stations.

It flows through overhead cables.

It flows through sub-stations in towns.

Mains electricity can kill people. Keep away from cables and sub-stations.

Inside buildings mains electricity flows through light switches.

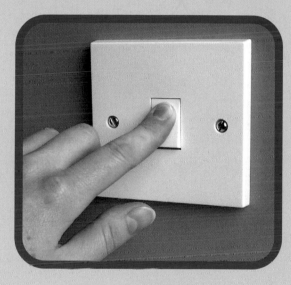

It flows through sockets.

Do not put your fingers in the sockets.

It flows through plugs and wires.

In the home

toaster

Electricity can be used in many ways. It can make heat and it can make things cold. It can make light and sound and it can make things move.

fridge

kettle

door bell

hair-dryer

iron

clock

food
mixer

desk lamp

fairy lights

radio

Here are some things that use electricity in the home. What do we use each one for? You can find some answers on the next page.

Sort them **out**

Someone has sorted the electrical things on pages 24 and 25 into groups.

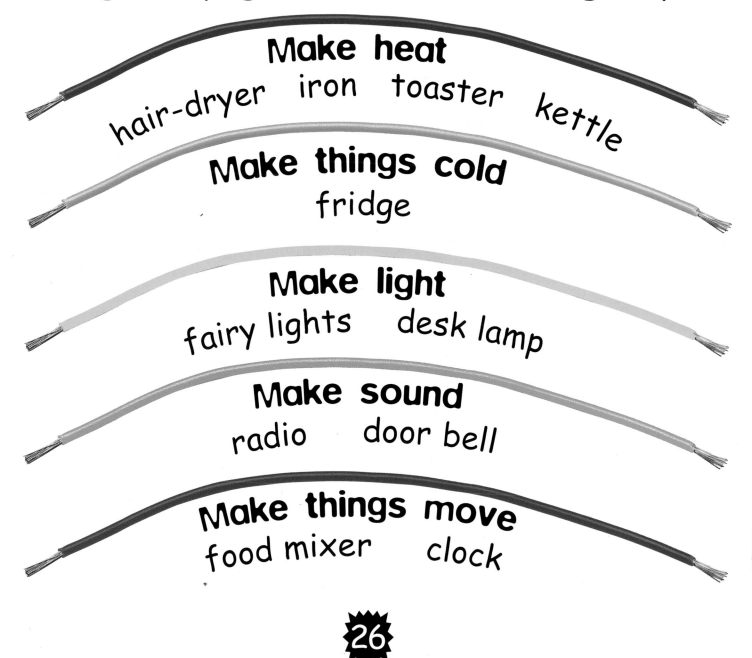

Make heat

hair-dryer   iron   toaster   kettle

Make things cold

fridge

Make light

fairy lights   desk lamp

Make sound

radio   door bell

Make things move

food mixer   clock

Here is a pictogram of these groups.

| heat | cold | light | sound | move |

Put the electrical things in your home into groups like these. Make a pictogram of the groups. Could any electrical things fit in more than one group?

Useful words

battery - a special cylinder or box which stores electricity. It can be used to make an electric circuit work.

buzzer - a part that makes a sound when electricity passes through it.

cable - a very thick wire which carries electricity from place to place. Cables may be underground or carried on pylons.

circuit - a complete circle around which electricity flows.

mains electricity - electricity that comes from plug sockets in the home.

motor - a part which makes something move when electricity passes through it.

plug - a part that is found on the end of a wire. It goes into a socket to power electrical objects.

power station - a place where electricity is made.

sub-station - a place where electricity moves from a thick cable to smaller cables to go into homes.

switch - a device which stops or starts the flow of electricity.

wire - a thin piece of metal, covered with plastic, that carries electricity.

Some answers

Here are some answers to the questions we have asked in this book. Don't worry if you had some different answers to ours; you may be right, too. Talk through your answers with other people and see if you can explain why they are right.

page 9   The plus and minus signs on the batteries and inside the toy help you to put the batteries back.

page 11   There are lots of different switches. Some you can push, like a light switch, and some you can twist, like on some radios.

page 15   You could always write down what happened, but a quick and easy way to record circuits is by drawing them. Here are two drawings showing Ben's circuit:

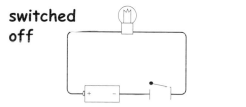

switched off

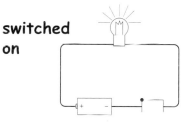

switched on

page 17   Here are some examples of machines with buzzers inside: clocks, smoke alarms, cookers and door bells.

page 21   You should check for gaps because the electricity will not flow if there is a gap in the circuit.

page 27   A toaster also moves when it pops up. Some fridges also have a light inside. Some clocks also make a 'tick-tock' sound. Lamps also give out heat – be careful not to touch them. A hair-dryer also has a motor inside that moves a fan.

Index

About this book

Ways into Science is designed to encourage children to begin to think about their everyday world in a scientific way, examining cause and effect through close observation, recording their results and discussing what they have seen. Here are some pointers to gain the maximum use from **Electricity**.

• Working through this book will introduce the basic concepts of electricity and also some of the language structures and vocabulary associated with it (for example, circuits, motors and switches, and comparatives such as bright and brighter). This will prepare the child for more formal work on electricity later in the school curriculum.

• The dangers of playing with mains electricity must be stressed. A warning occurs to this effect on page 7 and again on page 22 and 23.

• All experiments should be done with electricity from batteries such as those used to power toys. The experiments shown on pages 12, 13, 14 and 15 can be tried with simple apparatus under adult supervision.

• On pages 13, 19 and 25 children are invited to predict the results of a particular action or activity. Ensure you discuss the reason for any answer they give in some depth before turning over the page. Remember, in most situations, our solution is only one of several possibilities. Set up other scenarios for the children to predict and discuss possible outcomes as well.

• The circuits in the book have been laid out to show their components and connections clearly. As indicated by the question on page 15 and its answer on page 29, these can be used as a starting point for drawing circuit diagrams.